IMAGES
of America

GRAND TETON
NATIONAL PARK

In this image from the 1920s or 1930s, Harold Langland (left) is driving a touring car with passengers Muriel B. Olson (center) and Helen Langland. The trio is approaching Jenny Lake as the Grand Teton rises over Cascade Canyon in the background. As automobiles became more popular in the early 20th century, Grand Teton National Park experienced an increase in visitors on driving vacations. (Courtesy Jackson Hole Historical Society and Museum; photograph by Richard A. Olson.)

ON THE COVER: The dudes pictured here are riding horseback at the Triangle X Ranch. In 1926, John S. and Maytie Turner purchased a homestead on Spread Creek, a favorite vacation spot of theirs. They raised cattle and built a few cabins to accommodate hunters. The Turners purchased an adjacent homestead and expanded their property in 1928. They secured an operating lease when they sold to the Snake River Land Company in 1929. In 1950, the ranch was incorporated into Grand Teton National Park with a concession permit. It is the only concession-operated dude ranch in the national park system and the oldest remaining dude ranch in Jackson Hole. Turner family descendants continue to operate the ranch today. (Courtesy Jackson Hole Historical Society and Museum.)

IMAGES
of America

GRAND TETON
NATIONAL PARK

Kendra Leah Fuller and Shannon Sullivan
with images contributed by Jackson Hole Historical Society

ARCADIA
PUBLISHING

Published by Arcadia Publishing
Charleston, South Carolina

Printed in the United States of America

Library of Congress Control Number: 2013949752

For all general information, please contact Arcadia Publishing:
Telephone 843-853-2070
Fax 843-853-0044
E-mail sales@arcadiapublishing.com
For customer service and orders:
Toll-Free 1-888-313-2665

Visit us on the Internet at www.arcadiapublishing.com

*To those individuals who had the vision and perseverance to make
Grand Teton National Park a reality, preserving this national
treasure's spectacular beauty for future generations to enjoy.*

CONTENTS

ACKNOWLEDGMENTS

I would like to thank Shannon Sullivan for her countless hours scanning images and patience while I was researching and writing this manuscript. Without her collaboration in providing images, searching for just the right picture, and willingness to work across the miles, it would not have been possible to write about a subject so dear to my heart. To Clayton Caden, thank you for your time spent gathering research in anticipation of my visits and pointing me in the right direction. To the entire staff of the Jackson Hole Historical Society and Museum, thank you for your graciousness and hospitality. My time spent in your research center was invaluable in pulling this project together. Without your permission to access and use images from your archives, this book would not have been possible.

Thank you to Arcadia Publishing for providing me with the opportunity to write this book. To my editor, Jared Nelson, thank you for your help and guidance along the way. Your input was truly appreciated.

To my family, thank you for your willingness to take several research vacations. I know it was a hardship for you to go fishing, hiking, and rafting in such a beautiful place. Most importantly, thank you for your patience during the countless hours I spent researching and writing.

Unless otherwise noted, all images in this book appear courtesy of the Jackson Hole Historical Society and Museum.

INTRODUCTION

Every year, three million people journey to the northwest corner of Wyoming to visit Grand Teton National Park. These guests are rewarded with majestic views of rugged mountain peaks and glaciers that soar more than a mile over the valley floor of Jackson Hole and the winding Snake River. Crystal-clear rivers, streams, lakes, waterfalls, and abundant wildlife add to the allure of the park, drawing outdoorsmen, photographers, sightseers, and mountain climbers. Extraordinary measures were taken by many people over the years to ensure the park's preservation for the wildlife that depends on it and the people who come to bask in its beauty.

Today, some visitors might take the preservation of this mountain wilderness for granted, but this was not always the case. Modern park visitors may not be aware of the fight that resulted in this wilderness being designated a national park. Fortunately, the determination of conservationists, philanthropists, and visionaries who sought to protect the park prevailed. The United States owes these people a huge debt of gratitude for making it possible to still enjoy the pristine beauty of this land and its wildlife unspoiled by commercialization. Imagine how overrun and spoiled this land could have become if profiteers had been allowed to build hotels, restaurants, and housing developments all over the mountains and valley.

Although Grand Teton was designated a national park in 1929, the park as it exists today did not come about until its expansion in 1950. The path to making the area a national park was very long indeed. Gen. Philip Sheridan was one of the first to voice concern over the protection of the area. In 1882, Sheridan proposed that Yellowstone National Park be extended to include an area to the northern tip of Jackson Lake. In 1897, Yellowstone National Park superintendent Col. S.B.M. Young asked that Yellowstone officials be given jurisdiction over Jackson Hole to protect the elk herd from poachers outside of Yellowstone. Congress heard testimony over expansion in 1902, but no action was taken.

The first step toward Grand Teton becoming a national park came in 1915 when Secretary of the Interior Franklin K. Lane appointed Stephen Mather as his assistant in charge of national parks. Lane appointed Horace M. Albright to assist Mather, a pairing that united two individuals with great dedication to the conservation of the Tetons and Jackson Hole. The duo first laid eyes on the Tetons when they ventured south of Yellowstone's boundaries to Moran, Wyoming. The spectacular grandeur of the Teton Range came into view, and an undying love affair was born. Albright recognized that this splendor needed to be preserved forever, and he spent the next 35 years committed to making that preservation a reality.

In 1918, Albright, Mather, and Congressman Frank Mondell wrote a bill to extend the boundaries of Yellowstone to include the Teton Range, Jackson Lake and other lakes, the headwaters of the Yellowstone River at Two Ocean Pass, and the Buffalo Fork River. In February 1919, Mondell introduced a revised bill that passed the House unanimously; the general consensus was that it would be signed into law. Unfortunately, the bill met with opposition in the Senate from a group of Idaho sheep ranchers afraid they would lose their grazing rights, and the bill was killed.

This marked the beginning of the struggle between conservationists and the livestock owners, dude ranchers, and the US Forest Service (USFS). The USFS, which was opposed to the expansion of Yellowstone to include the Jackson Hole area, cut back livestock grazing area within the proposed expansion boundaries claiming concern for the local elk herd. Some speculated that this was intentionally done to rouse ranchers into opposition to the expansion. Regardless of the intentions of the USFS, the agency's action fueled the fires between the ranchers and the National Park Service (NPS).

Dude wranglers—led by Struthers Burt, one of the first dude wranglers in the valley—also opposed the expansion. Perhaps due to the remote isolation of Jackson Hole and the Tetons, the people who lived there were, on the whole, an independent group who resented perceived government interference. Although they were involved in the early tourism industry, they felt the pristine land they loved would become overrun with outsiders. They also worried about potential restrictions that could be placed upon them and feared overdevelopment of the area if the NPS took control of it.

Albright used his veto power to squelch plans to build a dam at the outlet of Jenny Lake for purposes of irrigation, an idea the USFS did not oppose. The irrigationists did not give up, and Albright vetoed their plans to dam Two Ocean and Emma Matilda Lakes. The vision the USFS held for the valley was at odds with Albright's vision of a preserved land. The USFS saw the land as a great resource that could be logged and mined; it proposed floating logs from the mountainsides across Jackson Lake to the Snake River, where they could be floated downstream, and claimed all this could be accomplished without harming the ecosystem of the area. The USFS was also in favor of expanding recreation areas and homes along the shores of Jackson Lake.

Even though they were on opposite sides of this debate, both Horace Albright and the dude wranglers were concerned about the preservation of the valley and its way of life. Albright's defense of the lakes won over the dude ranchers, and the forces joined together to protect Jackson Hole from development.

In 1925, Pres. Calvin Coolidge's Coordinating Commission on National Parks and Forests recommended that approximately 100,000 acres of the Grand Teton Range be added to Yellowstone National Park, not including any portion of the valley. Although this was far from what Stephen Mather and Albright had rallied for, they were happy to finally get some portion of the land incorporated into Yellowstone. The expansion was derailed when Sen. John Kendrick wanted the park named Teton National Park of Wyoming, since so many people mistakenly thought Yellowstone was located in Montana.

In 1928, public hearings were held in Jackson and Cody by the Senate Committee on Public Lands to determine local attitudes and ideas on park expansion. At the Jackson meeting, public sentiment supported a Grand Teton National Park proposal, as all but one person raised their hands in favor. The committee adjourned to the JY Ranch feeling that a victory was in hand. A group of businessmen and ranchers showed up late, claiming they had not known about the meeting, and convinced Senator Kendrick to have another meeting the following morning. There, the businessmen and ranchers voiced their opposition to the national park idea and recommended their own solutions. They eventually conceded but requested that no new hotels or camps be built within the park boundaries. Burt and Albright supported the idea and agreed that the bill would ban the construction of new roads, hotels, and camps.

On February 26, 1929, Pres. Calvin Coolidge signed the bill into law—Grand Teton National Park was born, although it only included the Teton Range and no portion of the valley. Although the conservationists had won national park status, it appeared inevitable that the lakes at the foot of the Tetons and Jackson Hole would be developed for tourists. Albright remained committed to his vision of a national park that incorporated Jackson Hole and persevered in his quest to make this vision a reality. The solution came through businessman and philanthropist John D. Rockefeller Jr., whom Albright had met with before winning this first battle.

Albright first met Rockefeller in 1924 during a tour of Yellowstone that he had arranged. In July 1926, Rockefeller and his family returned for a longer stay. During this second visit, Albright escorted them to Teton country. They were enamored with the beauty of the area and appalled by the commercialization that had already begun. Rockefeller's wife, Abigail, was very vocal about her disgust for the dance hall at Jenny Lake, along with other buildings and telephone wires that marred the landscape and disrupted the view. As the group traveled back to Yellowstone, Albright told Rockefeller about his efforts, struggles, and vision to preserve the entire valley.

After returning home, Rockefeller wrote to Albright requesting maps and property values of the private holdings in Jackson Hole. It appears that Albright misunderstood Rockefeller's request, for at their meeting, he only brought details on the properties west of the Snake River and south of Jenny Lake. Rockefeller instructed Albright to go back and obtain information on all the privately held properties in Jackson Hole and what it would cost to purchase them; he was only interested in Albright's complete vision of incorporating the entire valley into the national park.

Within days of receiving this information, Rockefeller signed on to Albright's grand plan. He instructed Col. Arthur Woods to write Albright with his intentions to purchase the entire Jackson Hole valley and eventually turn it over to the government to be managed by them as a national recreation area. Rockefeller placed Woods in charge of the project, because if his involvement and intentions were made public, the land values would become inflated. Rockefeller gave Woods the authority to purchase 14,170 acres on the west side of the Snake River and approximately 100,000 acres on the east side of the river in Jackson Hole for a total purchase price of around $1,397,000. It was Albright's suggestion to use a front company when purchasing the land, and all was to be done with the utmost secrecy.

The Snake River Land Company was incorporated under the guise of a recreation and hunting club. New York attorney Vanderbilt Webb was appointed president of the company. Albright suggested the Salt Lake City law firm of Fabian and Clendenin to handle the purchases, and Harold Fabian, an avid outdoorsman, was appointed vice president. Robert E. Miller, president of the Jackson State Bank, was chosen as the land purchasing agent even though he was personally against Albright's plans for the park. With Miller's stature as bank president, there was no way Albright and Rockefeller could avoid dealing with him—but they did so under subterfuge. Miller never knew the origin of the money backing the Snake River Land Company. He came on board as the purchasing agent in June 1927, stipulating that the small ranchers in the area be treated fairly when it came to the sale of their property.

Another hurdle that had to be cleared before purchasing could begin involved ensuring that government-owned land within the purchasing area would not be opened up to private purchase, as much of the land was still available under the Homestead Act of 1862. Kenneth Chorley, Rockefeller's chief agent at Colonial Williamsburg, met with Secretary of the Interior Hubert Work to explain Rockefeller and Albright's plan and the inevitable rise in valuation that would occur if the lands were still open to private individuals once purchasing began. The meeting resulted in President Coolidge signing an executive order for withdrawal of the land on July 7, 1927.

This executive order was met with much opposition and distrust from the Elk Commission, which had received another such order in April 1927 for expansion of the National Elk Refuge. The Elk Commission had promised Wyoming members there would be no requests to obtain more land in Jackson Hole. When President Coolidge signed the second order just months after these assurances, tempers flared. Chairman Charles Sheldon formally requested that the order be rescinded, and he was quickly joined by others. Afraid the order would indeed be rescinded, the Snake River Land Company went on the offensive and chose to let several congressmen in on their ultimate plans. Without revealing that Rockefeller was financing the plan, Vanderbilt Webb assured the congressmen that the land would be dedicated for use by the people, not held privately. This assuaged their fears, and the matter was closed.

Purchasing started anew. The Snake River Land Company acquired over 25,000 acres in Jackson Hole. Although the full extent of purchasing was not complete, Albright and Rockefeller felt they had enough land to request legislation expanding Grand Teton National Park. In April 1930, the Snake River Land Company issued a press release explaining the full involvement and intent of Rockefeller, Albright, and the National Park Service. This public revelation again fueled the fires of opposition.

Accusations arose about misdeeds on the part of the NPS, the General Land Office, and the Snake River Land Company. A senate investigative committee was formed, and hearings were held in Jackson. Sen. Robert Carey was intent on proving that all involved, particularly the Snake River Land Company, had used dubious methods to coerce landowners into selling their property. In fact, it was proven that other than a few small indiscretions, the parties had acted in an exemplary fashion. The matter of expanding the park was still not resolved.

By 1938, the legislative process had been ongoing for years, and it became apparent that a different plan of attack might yield better results. Albright and the others began seriously considering an idea that he had put forth years earlier to have the land declared a national monument by executive order. Rockefeller wrote to Harold Ickes, secretary of the interior, stating that if the government was not going to accept his gift of the land, then he would sell to private enterprise. This lit a fire under Ickes, who then took a meeting with Pres. Franklin D. Roosevelt.

On March 15, 1943, President Roosevelt signed Executive Order 2578 to establish the Jackson Hole National Monument. Another hurdle had been cleared and the players were ecstatic. Their joy was short-lived, though, as many felt that Roosevelt had overstepped his executive power and accused him of circumventing Congress. The media compared Roosevelt's executive order to Hitler's seizure of Austria. Bills were sponsored to abolish the monument. This prompted more investigative committees and hearings on the matter throughout the summer of 1943. Bill H.R. 2241 made it through the House and Senate but was vetoed by Roosevelt. The battle waged on through 1947, but the opposition had lost its momentum, and all bills died in committee.

Sentiment had swayed towards preservation. Influential conservation groups like the Sierra Club, National Audubon Society, Wilderness Society, and others joined forces to ensure the preservation of the park and monument. Times had changed, and by 1948, only a small group of ranchers and businessmen remained opposed to the National Park Service taking control of the area. In April 1949, a conference between the NPS and the people of Teton County allowed each side to reach an amicable compromise. The NPS conceded grazing rights and reimbursement for lost property tax revenue; the organization also established an advisory committee to decide the best management of the elk herd.

With the park expansion finally moving forward in a positive manner, Rockefeller deeded the remaining 33,562 acres of land he owned to the federal government with the stipulation that if the lands were used for any purpose other than public parks, they would automatically revert back to Jackson Hole Preserve Inc., a nonprofit organization founded by Rockefeller and led by his son Laurance. The government accepted Rockefeller's gift at a ceremony on December 16, 1949. On April 12, 1950, Sen. Joseph A. Mahoney introduced a bill to the Senate that resolved the remaining issues and incorporated the Jackson Hole National Monument into an expanded Grand Teton National Park. After a 68-year preservation battle, Pres. Harry Truman signed the bill establishing the modern Grand Teton National Park on September 13, 1950.

One

A Changing Landscape

The spectacular way the Teton Range vertically soars above the valley of Jackson Hole often inspires wonder about how the landscape was created. The Grand Teton stands over 7,000 feet above Jackson Hole. Unlike most mountain ranges, the Tetons lack foothills and rise steeply from the valley floor. The Teton Range is one of the youngest ranges in the Rocky Mountains. Most ranges in the Rockies formed over 50 million years ago, but the uplift that created the Teton Range began just 10 million years ago when the stretching of the earth's crust pulled two tectonic plates away from each other, creating the Teton Fault.

The fault extends 40 miles along the east side of the Teton Range between the mountains and the valley floor. Continued tension between the plates and heat from the Yellowstone hotspot fractured the earth's crust, causing earthquakes. The valley crust began dropping beneath the plate to the west, forcing the crust on the west side of the fault skyward at the rate of about 10 feet per quake. This continued over the course of millions of years, eventually forming the Teton Range. Seismic activity is ongoing, and the mountains are still being lifted as the valley floor continues to tilt and sink beneath the opposing plate.

Ancient seas, volcanic activity, glaciers, and landslides have also played a part in shaping the landscape of Grand Teton National Park. Fossilized evidence of ancient seas and lakes can be seen on the highest peaks of the Tetons. Approximately two million years ago, earth entered the Pleistocene Ice Age, which started a cycle of vast ice sheets flowing through the region from Yellowstone followed by interglacial periods of warming that allowed the glaciers to retreat and vegetation to spread. As the glaciers moved through the area, they gouged the valley and deposited glacial moraines. As the glaciers melted, these moraines dammed the water to form the beautiful valley lakes that exist today. Today, there are still 12 glaciers in the Teton Range, but they are slowly disappearing.

Mount Moran rises to 12,605 feet and displays Skillet Glacier, the most prominent glacier in the park. The summit is 6,000 feet above Jackson Lake, and the mountain is home to four other glaciers. The black dike left of the "skillet handle" was formed by cooling magma. The dike is 150 feet thick and extends over seven miles through the mountain to the west. Mount Moran is the only peak that still shows evidence of flathead sandstone (visible to the right of the dike in the image below) formed by pre-Cambrian seas depositing sediments some 500 million years ago. (Both photographs by Kendra Fuller.)

The Cathedral Group holds eight of the ten tallest peaks in the park. The most common peaks referred to in the Cathedral Group are, from left to right, Middle Teton (12,804 feet), Grand Teton (13,770 feet), and Mount Owen (12,928 feet). Other peaks in this group include South Teton, Teepe Pillar, Teewinot Mountain, Buck Mountain, and Nez Perce Peak. (Photograph by Harrison Crandall.)

Petersen Glacier and Mica Lake are located above Cascade Canyon. The glacier is named after Frank Petersen, a climber from the first documented ascent of the Grand Teton in 1898. Petersen Glacier is no longer visible in satellite imagery, indicating that it may have disappeared. With current climate trends, scientists have estimated that more Teton glaciers will disappear by the middle of the 21st century. (Photograph by Frederick Pilcher.)

Climber Paul Petzoldt peers into a deep crevasse on Teton Glacier in 1933. Teton Glacier, the largest glacier in the park, is located on the north face of the Grand Teton between Grand Teton and Mount Owen. The glacier moves at a rate of 30 feet per year and has lost 20 percent of its mass over the last 50 years. (Photograph by Frank Smith.)

This glacial ice field is just a small remnant of the glacial ice that once flowed through Jackson Hole from the Greater Yellowstone Glacial System. Glacial ice over 3,000 feet thick scoured the mountains and valley, gouging out the region's jagged landscape and lakes. (Courtesy of Mr. & Mrs. Harold P. Fabian.)

The Death Canyon Shelf (9,500 feet) is composed of limestone deposited beneath an ancient Cambrian sea 500 million years ago. The shelf (pictured at right) is located above Phelps Lake and Death Canyon and is a 10-mile hike from the nearest trailhead. It is a narrow plateau that extends almost four miles between Fox Creek Pass and Mount Meek Pass. Fossilized horn corals (below), brachiopods, and gastropods can be found on the shelf and high up in the Teton Range, proving that the range was buried beneath a sea before the upheaval that began around 10 million years ago. (Right, photograph by Kendra Fuller; below, courtesy National Park Service.)

This photograph looks down on Bradley and Taggart Lakes from Glacier Trail. During the Pinedale glaciation period, which lasted for approximately 20,000 years (between 10,000 and 30,000 years ago), glacial ice flowed out of high mountain canyons and deposited moraines. As temperatures warmed, the glacial ice melted and filled in the moraines, creating the area's beautiful lakes. (Photograph by Harrison Crandall.)

The mountains average 450 inches of snow every year, while the valley floor averages 168 inches. Teton Pass, located just south of the park at an elevation of 8,431 feet, connects Jackson Hole with Victor, Idaho. Several avalanche slide paths cross the road, and it is often closed in the mornings for avalanche observation and control. (Photograph by J. Thralls.)

Passengers Ted Major, Jim Huidekoper, and 12-year-old Bobby MacLeod were in this jeep when it was caught in an avalanche on December 14, 1946. They were traveling on the old Teton Pass Road when Glory Bowl slid. Major revisited the scene a day later and took this photograph.

In February 1930, Harry Swanson perished in the Crater Lake slide below Glory Bowl. He was in the timber business and lived in a cabin near the lake with the group of men pictured here. They were unsuccessful in digging him out, and his body could not be recovered until the following spring.

The Gros Ventre landslide occurred seven miles east of the park on the north face of Sheep Mountain, in the Gros Ventre Wilderness area of Bridger-Teton National Forest. On June 23, 1925, approximately 50 million cubic yards of mostly sedimentary rock slid down the mountain after a heavy snow pack melt, heavy rains, and possible earthquake tremors.

When the mountain broke loose, the rock field crossed the Gros Ventre River and continued approximately 300 feet up the opposing mountainside. The rock became a dam over 200 feet high and 400 yards across the river, creating a new lake (Lower Slide Lake) that was five miles long. (Photograph by Guil Huff.)

After the Gros Ventre landslide on June 23, 1925, rancher Guil Huff (above) climbed atop a roof to survey the damage to his property. Longtime resident William Bierer sold his property to Huff in 1920, predicting a landslide would occur. On the afternoon of the event, Huff set off on horseback to investigate loud rumblings in the distance. He witnessed the huge mass of debris coming towards him and narrowly escaped its path by 20 feet. Rocks and trees tumbled down the mountain at 50 mph and covered 17 acres of Huff's ranch. By the following morning, his land was covered in water from the leaking dam, and by June 29, the house was lost to the lake (below).

Scenes at the Great Landslide

Sudden Lake, formed by Gros Ventre landslide and then drained by the washout two years later; taken July 1925

Gros Ventre landslide taken from north side of Valley July 1925

Horsetail Ranger Station, floating in Sudden Lake and moored to shore

Hit by the slide where the Huff place once was.

A ranch home surrounded by driftwood

A 1925 issue of *Midwest Review Magazine* included these photographs of the Gros Ventre landslide. Mother Nature only took three minutes to forever change the landscape. The slide was a major geological event. Aside from volcanic eruptions, it was one of the largest landmass movements in Earth's recent history.

After the June 1925 landslide, water below the new natural dam was five feet deep and ran just beneath the Grovont Bridge at the town of Kelly. Unlike a man-made dam, there was no spillway to prevent overflow or erosion; however, the dam was declared safe by engineers and scientists who inspected it. This steel truss bridge was wiped out when the dam broke during a flood in 1927.

In the c. 1920 image above, a horse-drawn wagon awaits its owner in front of the Kelly Mercantile building. After floodwaters from the landslide took out his ranger station, US Forest Service ranger Charles Dibble remained leery of the dam and moved his family to Kelly. From Kelly, he kept a watchful eye on the dam. The dam made it through the spring runoff of 1926, and many people stopped worrying about it. Before the 1927 flood, the Gros Ventre River flowed into the town of Kelly with plenty of clearance beneath the Gros Ventre Bridge, as shown below.

In this 1927 photograph, floodwater is surging beneath the Gros Ventre Bridge at Kelly. The winter of 1926–1927 was one of the worst on record. Heavy rains arrived in spring, quickly melting the deep snow pack. The Gros Ventre River rose, spilling water over the natural dam on May 17, 1927. Ranger Charles Dibble, Frank Ellis, and others were working near the Kelly bridge when Dibble noticed a hayrack, which had been in the lake above the dam since the 1925 landslide, floating down the river. Dibble and Ellis jumped into his Model T and raced upriver to inspect the situation. The top 60 feet of the dam had given way, and they were met with a raging torrent of water and debris heading toward Kelly. They sped back to town, but residents had just 15 minutes to flee to safety. The wall of water grew as high as 50 feet as it carried trees, boulders, and debris through the valley. The town of Kelly was almost completely decimated—only three buildings remained standing. Even with Dibble and Ellis's warning, six people perished in the flood.

Two

EARLY HUMAN INHABITANTS

With the close of the Pinedale Glaciation Period approximately 10,000 years ago, plants and wildlife began to emerge in the park. Archaeological evidence shows that the earliest human inhabitants seasonally made homes in the park area approximately 11,000 years ago. Amateur archaeologist W.C. "Slim" Lawrence was a local ranch caretaker with a passion for collecting artifacts found in Grand Teton National Park. Lawrence collected artifacts for 30 years starting in the 1930s. His collection, which numbered in the thousands, was a primary contributor to those attempting to assemble an idea of prehistoric life in the park. In the 1970s, professional archaeologist Gary Wright, from University at Albany, State University of New York, gathered associates to investigate the area and formed a hypothesis about the prehistoric people of the region.

The nomadic Paleo-Indians who resided in the Grand Teton National Park area were primarily hunter-gatherers who arrived in northern Jackson Hole in early spring to harvest edible and medicinal plants and roots in the valley. They established base camps at the northern end of Jackson Lake. There they built roasting pits, fished in the lake with nets, and hunted for bison, elk, mule deer, and bighorn sheep. As temperatures warmed the higher elevations during the summer months, they followed the ripening plants up the mountainsides to continue harvesting and exited the valley into Idaho before the harsh winters arrived.

Materials used in the making of ancient artifacts found in the park provide clues about the migratory patterns of the Paleo-Indians. Obsidian, volcanic glass formed by rapidly cooling lava, was a popular material used to make tools. Each volcanic flow has unique elements, which allows scientists to date obsidian artifacts and reveal their sources. As glaciers gouged the valley, obsidian outcroppings were revealed in Jackson Hole, Yellowstone National Park, and other areas. Most artifacts found in the park come from an obsidian source known as the Teton Pass source at the southern end of the Teton range. Based on this evidence, it is thought that the Paleo-Indians entered Jackson Hole at the southern end near Teton Pass then continued on to the northern end of Jackson Lake.

Amateur archaeologist W.C. "Slim" Lawrence stands next to a prehistoric fire hearth he discovered in 1937. The hearth was revealed during a period of low water along the eastern shore of Jackson Lake.

The roasting pits pictured here during a low-water period in 1986 are the oldest discovered in the park. They are located at the Lawrence Site on the north shore of Jackson Lake and are carbon dated to the Early Archaic period (5,000 to 8,000 years ago). Early inhabitants gathered quartzite cobbles to fill the pits upon which a fire was built, then used the pits like ovens to roast root plants and to perform bone grease processing for winter food storage. These pits were used from year to year, and scientists now believe that some prehistoric people may have wintered in the park.

Archaeologist Gary Wright theorized that Early Archaic people spent early summer in the park at lower elevations, forming base camps along the shores of Jackson Lake. They gathered food in the valleys and fished in the lake, as shown by these fishing net weights from the W.C. Lawrence Collection. These and other artifacts, along with the roasting pits on Jackson Lake, support Wright's theory.

In the Early Archaic period, mano and metate grinding stones—such as these artifacts from the W.C. Lawrence Collection—were used to grind various plant leaves, roots, seeds, berries, and flowers (like the blue camas bulbs in the picture) for use in various foods and medicines. The mano (the smaller, light-colored rock) was typically made of sandstone and was rolled back and forth across the flat rock known as a metate.

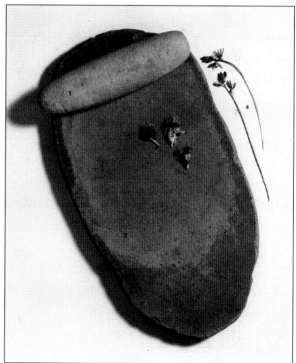

Steatite bowls from the W.C. Lawrence collection date to the Late Prehistoric period (1,500 to 500 years ago). Steatite, or soapstone, was a soft rock that was carved with an elk antler or other tool then hardened by fire. The Late Prehistoric period was marked by dramatic changes and innovation in sustenance and hunting apparatuses, from the spear and atlatl to bow and arrow. (Photograph by Olie Riniker.)

These various hammerstones were found at the W.C. Lawrence site in Grand Teton National Park. Hammerstones were used to make projectile points, such as spearheads, and other tools by striking the hammerstone against a rock until it was fashioned into the desired tool. Obsidian was a popular choice for items requiring a sharp edge. (Photograph by Olie Riniker.)

The oldest projectiles in the W.C. Lawrence collection date back 9,000 years to the Paleo-Indian period. Stone spear points attached to a wooden shaft were thrown by hand or with an atlatl (spear thrower). The atlatl increased speed and distance by acting as an extension of the throwing arm. This hunting method was used until 2,000 years ago, when the bow and arrow was devised. (Photograph by Olie Riniker.)

In this image, W.C. "Slim" Lawrence is standing in front of Ed Trafton's hideout cabin. Trafton held up stagecoaches in Wyoming and Idaho and was a known horse thief, cattle rustler, and robber. He frequented the Jackson Hole area from 1881 to 1915. His hideout cabin was so well hidden in the Teton forest that it was not discovered until Lawrence found it in 1931.

W.C. "Slim" Lawrence is pictured in his living room with part of his artifact collection in the 1930s or 1940s. Lawrence was a ranch caretaker who began collecting artifacts he found in the park and Jackson Hole during the 1930s. He was an avid collector, and his collection grew over the next 30 years to include thousands of artifacts and discoveries. Although some of his finds were made while he was out hunting or trapping with his wife, Verba, the pair made regular trips by horse and on foot to hunt for artifacts. They particularly liked to take morning expeditions to Jackson Lake, where they explored the lake's shores on foot. At the urging of Verba, who felt the collection was taking over their house and property, he partnered with Homer Richards in 1958 and opened the Jackson Hole Museum to house his collection. The museum was located in the town of Jackson, and Lawrence's collection is still housed there today at the Jackson Hole Historical Society and Museum at 225 North Cache Street.

Three

PIONEERS OF EXPLORATION

Exploration of Jackson Hole and the Teton Range began in the early 1800s. The fur trade was booming, which fueled the desires of businessmen like Manuel Lisa and John Jacob Astor to expand their empires westward. They established trading posts and sent explorers through Jackson Hole in search of a route to the rich trading grounds of the Pacific Northwest. The Teton Range became a well-known landmark for trappers and traders, and Jackson Hole became a crossroads of this activity. French speaking trappers christened the range Les Trois Tetons (The Three Breasts), while Wilson Price Hunt, of the Astorians, referred to them as the Pilot Knobs.

In 1807, Lisa, owner of the Missouri Fur Company, sent John Colter from his trading post in present-day Montana to Idaho to establish trade with the Crow Indians. Colter is believed to be the first white settler to see the Tetons, although his exact route is disputed. Lisa's partner, Andrew Henry, and his crew of trappers were the first white settlers to put traps in the rivers and streams in the valley in 1810. In 1811, Astor, owner of the American Fur Company, sent representatives known as the Astorians to establish a route for a trading post on the Columbia River. Robert Stuart and Hunt led the Astorians through Jackson Hole. By the 1830s, energies switched from exploration to trapping the streams and rivers of the mountains and valley.

In 1860, the federal government began to perform surveys to establish the best route for a transcontinental railroad. The Raynolds Expedition, guided by trapper Jim Bridger, was the first to enter Jackson Hole for this purpose. Capt. William F. Raynolds deemed the route unsuitable for a railroad. Two less notable surveys followed. Then, a member of Raynolds's original entourage, Ferdinand Vandiveer Hayden, returned to undertake the Hayden Geological Surveys in the 1870s. This era of surveys mapped the area and resulted in the naming of many of the Teton mountains, passes, and lakes.

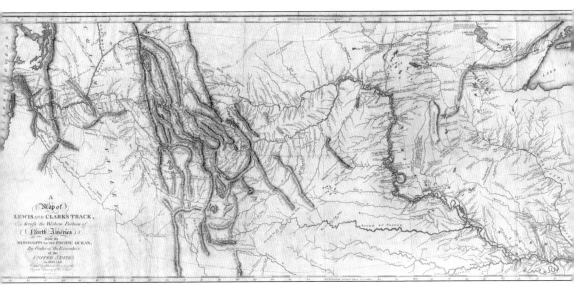

An adventurer at heart, John Colter first ventured west in 1804 when he enlisted with the Lewis and Clark Expedition, which set out from St. Louis to chart a water route to the Pacific coast under the direction of Pres. Thomas Jefferson. In 1807, Colter met and worked for Manuel Lisa at a trading post at the confluence of the Yellowstone and Bighorn Rivers. Lisa employed Colter to travel west and inform the Crow Indians of the trading post. It is thought that he traveled through Jackson Hole and crossed the Teton Range during the winter of 1807–1808. Although Colter is credited with being the first white man to venture into Jackson Hole, his exact route was not charted at the time. Instead, in 1810 he recounted his journey to Gen. William Clark, who charted it on the map above, which was published in 1814 in *History Of The Expedition Under The Command Of Captains Lewis And Clark, To The Sources Of The Missouri, Thence Across The Rocky Mountains And Down The River Columbia To The Pacific Ocean.*

The Colter Stone was found in 1930 outside of Tetonia, Idaho. Sixteen-year-old William Richard Beard unearthed the stone while plowing his father's field. The stone is carved into the shape of a skull with Colter's name and the year 1808 engraved on either side. Most historians agree on its authenticity, and some feel it provides proof that Colter did indeed cross the Tetons on his journey.

Here, tourists gather near the Colter Monument at Colter Bay. The inscription on the stone reads: "This bay is named for John Colter, discoverer of the Teton Mountains and scenic wonders of the Upper Yellowstone. Experienced as a hunter for the 1804–1806 Lewis and Clark Expedition, he explored this region in winter of 1807–1808 in the employ of fur trader Manuel Lisa. Dedicated on the 150th anniversary of Colter's historic passage. 1957."

Artifacts from the fur trade on display at the Jackson Hole Historical Society and Museum include a trap used by Beaver Dick Leigh (upper left) and a Sharps rifle used by Dead Shot Swenson (upper right). Beaver pelts were so popular in the early 1800s that the animals were almost hunted to extinction.

Other items in the Jackson Hole Historical Society and Museum collection include a trap used by Beaver Dick Leigh's one-time employer, the Hudson's Bay Company (upper right); hatchets (left) and bullet-molding equipment (lower right). These items would have been used by Teton trappers such as Davey Jackson, William Sublette, and Jedediah Smith, a famous explorer of the American West who discovered South Pass, which became the main route for pioneers on the Oregon Trail through southwest Wyoming.

This portrait of trapper David E. "Davey" Jackson was commissioned during his service in the War of 1812 under Pres. Andrew Jackson, a distant relative. He was also the uncle of Gen. "Stonewall" Jackson. In 1822, he answered a call in a St. Louis newspaper advertisement by Gen. William Ashley and became one of "Ashley's Hundred," along with Jedediah Smith and William Sublette. Ashley and his partner, Maj. Andrew Henry, were looking for 100 men to ascend the Missouri River to its source for the purpose of establishing a fur-trading operation. In 1826, Jackson, Smith, and Sublette bought out Ashley and Henry. William Sublette named the Teton valley "Jackson's Hole," as it was one of Jackson's favorite places to trap beaver. The name was later changed to Jackson Hole. In 1830 they sold the business, and it became known as the Rocky Mountain Fur Company. More American trappers followed on the heels of their success to compete with British fur companies. By 1840 the trapping grounds had been depleted and the industry drastically declined, marking the end of the fur trade era.

Trapper and explorer Jim Bridger (pictured at left) served as a guide for the first government survey for a transcontinental railroad. The Raynolds Expedition, commanded by Capt. W.F. Raynolds, left Fort Pierre, South Dakota, on June 18, 1859. Bridger led the expedition through the Badlands and Black Hills of South Dakota into Wyoming. On May 31, 1860, they crossed the Continental Divide between the Gros Ventre and Wind River Mountains. Raynolds named the crossing—which was also used by the Astorians in 1811—Union Pass. In 1844, Bridger carved his name into a rock (below) at Names Hill, a place that contains many names of Oregon Trail travelers. The date shows his prior familiarity with the territory through which he guided the expedition. In 1964, the Wilderness Act, passed by Congress and signed into law by Pres. Lyndon B. Johnson, designated the Bridger Wilderness to memorialize this famous mountain man.

This group of men resting in front of a fireplace in a cabin on Sawtell's Ranch in Fremont County, Idaho, includes members of the Hayden Expedition of 1871–1872. In the 1870s, Ferdinand Vandiveer Hayden, a member of the Raynolds Expedition, spearheaded three government surveys into Yellowstone and Jackson Hole. (Photograph by William Henry Jackson.)

Part of Hayden's entourage gathered for this picture. Hayden's men split into two divisions—Hayden set out to survey Yellowstone, contributing to it becoming a national park later that year, while James Stevenson led the Snake River Division to Teton Basin, Idaho. After reconnecting with Hayden, Stevenson ventured south to survey the Snake River area. He rejoined with guide Beaver Dick Leigh at the inlet to Jackson Lake. (Photograph by William Henry Jackson.)

Beaver Dick Leigh is pictured above with his first family. They are, from left to right, Beaver Dick; Anne Jane; John; Beaver Dick's wife, Jenny, holding William and pregnant with daughter Elisabeth; and Richard Jr. Born in England, Leigh stowed away on a ship to America at 16. He found employment with the Hudson's Bay Company and later settled on the western side of the Tetons. He spent his life trapping in the Tetons and guided the Hayden Expedition of 1872. The expedition named Leigh and Jenny Lakes after Dick and his wife. In 1876, after taking in a woman sick with smallpox, Beaver Dick's entire family succumbed to the disease. He later married Susan Tadpole, a Bannock Indian promised to him when he aided in her birthing. His second family is pictured below. From left to right are Susan, William Bradhurst, Rose (on her father's lap), and Emma.

As part of the Snake River Division, William Henry Jackson was the first photographer to take pictures of the Tetons. These photographs were taken from Pierre's Hole, or Teton Basin, on the west side of the Teton Range. After the division met up with Hayden in Yellowstone, Jackson did not continue on to Jackson Hole, so there were no photographs taken from the east side of the mountains. Jackson later returned with the Hayden Expedition of 1878 to take the first photographs of the Tetons from Jackson Hole; he entered the valley at the south end in the Hoback Mountains and traveled north through Jackson Hole into Yellowstone.

PHOTOGRAPHING IN HIGH PLACES

William Henry Jackson (crouching) and his assistant, Charles Campbell, traveled from Teton Basin across treacherous terrain and snowpack to the summit of Table Mountain. This is where Jackson took the first pictures of the Tetons from the Idaho side. While Jackson was on a photographic excursion in 1872, the rest of the Snake River Division was busy surveying and mapping the Teton Range. During their stay, James Stevenson and Nathaniel Pitt Langford reportedly made the first ascent of the Grand Teton. Whether they actually reached the summit came under dispute on August 11, 1898, when William O. Owen, Franklin Spalding, John Shive, and Frank Petersen made the first documented ascent of the Grand Teton; they found no evidence—such as items left behind—to suggest any humans had been there before. The debate over who actually reached the summit first still rages today.

Thomas Moran, pictured at right in 1876, was a member of the 1872 Hayden Expedition who went on to become a famous artist. He traveled through Yellowstone with Hayden but did not go to Jackson Hole with the Snake River Division. In 1879, he traveled to Teton Basin to see the mountain named after him. His sketch below, titled *The Tetons*, is from the western vantage point. During his time in Yellowstone, Moran created over 30 sketches of the area. The creation of Yellowstone National Park in 1872 was due in part to the abilities of Moran and photographer William Henry Jackson. Moran's 1872 painting, *The Grand Canyon of the Yellowstone*, was purchased by the government for $10,000. Another of his paintings, *The Three Tetons*, now hangs in the Oval Office. (Below, courtesy National Park Service.)

In addition to naming Mount Moran (above) after artist Thomas Moran, the Snake River Division of the 1872 Hayden Expedition named many lakes and peaks in the valley. Many of these names came from members of the expedition. The group attempted to rename the Grand Teton "Mount Hayden," but the new name did not endure. Mount St. John was named for Oreste St. John, a field geologist who accompanied the surveys in 1877 and 1878. In addition to naming Jenny and Leigh Lakes after Beaver Dick Leigh and his wife, they named several other glacial lakes and streams in the park, including Taggart, Bradley, and Phelps Lakes. Notable people from the expeditions went on to become prominent figures in their fields, including botanist John Merle Coulter and naturalist Clinton Hart Merriam, one of the original founders of the National Geographic Society. These important expeditions provided the first accurate topographical maps of Grand Teton National Park and the surrounding area. (Photograph by Kendra Fuller.)

Four

THE QUEST FOR GOLD

In 1849, following the discovery of gold at Sutter's Mill in California, prospectors spread across the West hoping to strike it rich. By 1858, gold had been discovered in Nevada and the Rocky Mountains of Colorado. After gold was discovered in Bannock City and Virginia City, Montana, in 1862 and 1863, respectively, prospectors turned to the Grand Teton Range and Jackson Hole.

Walter W. DeLacey led the first group of prospectors to the Grand Tetons in search of gold, setting out with 25 fellow prospectors on August 7, 1863, from the Beaverhead River in Montana after they elected DeLacey their captain. The group was joined by another 16 men, and on August 22, they became the first prospectors to place pans in Jackson Hole waters on the Hoback River. The men found plenty of color but nothing substantial and continued on through the valley to Pacific Creek, where they established a base camp and split into four parties to prospect the surrounding area. DeLacey led his group north to the Jackson Lake inlet of the Snake River. Again, they found some color but no mother lode.

DeLacey produced a map of the area in 1865, and the journey has become more well known for its exploration of the area than for locating gold. In 1876, DeLacey published an account of the expedition in which he stated that the prospectors met no other people in the valley nor did they find any trapper cabins, homesteads, camps, or Indian villages. This suggests that the Teton valley was basically abandoned after the close of the fur-trapping era in the early 1840s. Most prospectors left the Tetons when they did not strike it rich. A few, like John Carnes, stayed to become some of the first settlers in the valley.

This man is panning for gold on the edge of a Teton stream. Panning is the oldest method of gold mining. After locating a placer deposit, such as this streambed, gravel and sand are scooped into the pan and gently swirled around, which allows the heavier gold to sink to the bottom. This method was often used by prospectors to locate the source of the placer deposit.

These prospectors are shoveling gravel and sand from a placer deposit into a sluice box. As water flowed through the sluice box, particles would be moved along the length of the box and the heavier gold particles would be trapped in the bottom by riffles, strips of wood or metal. Water was often directed into the box with a long wooden flume.

This waterwheel is being fed by a downward-sloping wooden flume. As mining equipment progressed, the waterwheel was used to provide power to mining operations. In underground mining, there may have been many waterwheels used to lift seeping water from one level to another up the mineshaft to keep the work area dry.

Miners Frank Coffin, Don Graham, and Jim Webb are searching through silt at their mine on Pacific Creek. They later abandoned this claim because the gold could not be retrieved. In 1909, Coffin took up a homestead on the Buffalo Fork River; he worked for the Triangle X dude ranch for most of his life. (Photograph by William Balderston.)

The miner at right is wearing a hat fitted with a carbide lamp used for illuminating underground tunnels, and another lamp dangles in his hand. Not all mining in the Teton Range was done above ground. Some prospectors dug tunnels in the mountains on quests for gold. When it became apparent that gold was not going to be found in large quantities, other mining operations, such as talc and asbestos, took over.

The opening of the mineshaft remained visible after a cave-in around 1932 at this asbestos mine on Berry Creek on the western side of Jackson Lake.

John Graul built a mining shack (left) and a cabin (below) in Webb Canyon on the west side of Jackson Lake. Every spring, after snowmelt, Graul returned to work on his tunnel. He managed to cut a tunnel 193 feet long before his death in a Colorado mining accident; no one knows for sure what he was seeking. W.C. Lawrence believed that Graul was tunneling for platinum. Lawrence owned an asbestos claim in the nearby canyon of Berry Creek. In 1914, the Reclamation Service developed the first coal mines from a coal field 60 miles long on the eastern side of Jackson Hole. The coal was used to power the Jackson Lake Dam. Other coal mines were developed and served the local market until the 1940s. There is no longer any coal mining in Jackson Hole.

Karl "Uncle Jack" Davis (center, with his hand on his chest) stands next to his pack horse with a group of prospectors. Davis came to the valley in the 1880s to seek his fortune after working in the goldfields of Montana. He staked a claim in the Snake River Canyon and built a cabin near Bailey Creek. (Photograph by Al Austin.)

In Jackson Hole, Davis devoted his life to finding gold and listed his occupation as gold miner on the 1900 census. Like many other prospectors of the time, his dream never materialized. When he died in 1911, he only had about $12 in gold amalgam to his name. (Photograph by Al Austin.)

The mining cutback pictured above is on the bank of the Snake River and is still visible today. If gold had been discovered in the Jackson Hole area, the destructive scarring that would have occurred would have demolished the landscape. The foundation of a prospector's cabin still exists in upper Death Canyon along with small tunnels that were dug into the mountainside by someone in search of gold. Similar tunnels exist in Avalanche Canyon. Although no one ever found a mother lode of gold near the Grand Tetons, companies mined other minerals, like talc and asbestos. If the area had not been designated a national park, the mining of these resources may have gone unchecked and forever altered this pristine wilderness. The photograph below shows Bill Hutton and his dog at the entrance to a talc mine on Owl Creek. (Below, photograph by W.C. Lawrence.)

Five

OUTLAWS AND THE OLD WEST

Despite the romantic notion that a valley surrounded by mountains would have been the perfect hideout for all sorts of scallywags, life in the shadow of the Grand Tetons was rather peaceful and lawful. In the late 1800s, the discovery of gold throughout the Rocky Mountains beckoned a new breed of explorers and gold and land prospectors who brought greed along with them. Greed was the common theme in two suspicious, deadly incidents in the late 1800s.

In the Story of Deadman's Bar, John Tonnar allegedly murdered his three prospecting partners by shooting one in the back and killing the others with ax blows to their heads. He was acquitted, but questions still surround this mystery. Why did he not have any horses when he arrived at Emile Wolff's ranch? There was never any gold found, yet a half-mile-long sluice has been found at the site. Why would someone go to the trouble of building the sluice if there was no gold?

Mystery also surrounds the death of Robert Ray Hamilton, who traveled to Wyoming after being duped by his wife. Hamilton became land partners with John D. Sargent. Months after Hamilton's arrival, he went hunting and never returned. Hamilton's body was found in the Snake River and ruled a drowning. Some speculated that Hamilton faked his death, while others claimed that Sargent murdered him.

Horse thieves and cattle rustlers used the protected basin to drive herds stolen from Idaho and Montana. Perhaps the most infamous rustler was "Teton" Jackson, who drove stolen herds to the basin from 1878 through 1885. Following Jackson's example, a pair of horse thieves from Montana thought the valley would be an ideal place to hide their stolen goods. The shoot-out that ensued became known as the Affair at Cunningham's Ranch. Yet another horse thief, Ed Trafton, was Teton Valley's first postman, but he became famous for robbing stagecoaches in Yellowstone. Many tales from the Old West have been exaggerated over time, but perhaps the quickest exaggeration occurred over the telegraph wires and turned a fairly small incident into the Bannock War of 1895.

The above image shows a group of men at a mining camp. With the discovery of gold throughout the Rocky Mountains in 1863, prospectors looked to the Tetons to make their fortunes. Prospectors John Tonnar, T.H. Tiggerman, August Kellenberger, and Henry Welter arrived in the summer of 1886. They staked a claim on the Snake River, near the Snake River Overlook. Later that summer, the bodies of Tiggerman, Kellenberger, and Welter were discovered in the river. Lone survivor John Tonnar was arrested by a posse. At his trial for murder in Evanston, he claimed self-defense; since there were no witnesses to the crime, he was acquitted. Questions still surround this tale of frontier murder known as the Story of Deadman's Bar (pictured below). (Above, photograph by Horace Albright; below, courtesy Stephen Leek Collection, American Heritage Center, University of Wyoming.)

Pierce Cunningham's cabin was the site of the shoot-out known as the Affair at Cunningham's Ranch. In the fall of 1892, Cunningham was approached by George Spenser and Mike Burnett. They needed hay for their horses and a place to stay. Cunningham allowed them to winter in his cabin by Spread Creek. Word of his guests traveled to Montana, where the two were wanted horse thieves, and locals formed a posse that stormed the cabin in April 1893. The fugitives were awakened by their barking dog in the early morning hours. A shoot-out ensued, leaving both fugitives dead. They were buried in unmarked graves beside the cabin. The posse claimed it was not their intent to kill the fugitives, but rumors spread that two locals had previously been asked to dispose of the thieves.

Robert Ray Hamilton, a remittance man and a great-grandson of Alexander Hamilton, arrived in the valley in May 1890. There he met John D. Sargent, who had settled on Jackson Lake, and the two became land partners. Hamilton had left behind a scandalous affair in New York in which he had married a woman who claimed to have given birth to his child; he soon found out she was already married and had purchased the child from a midwife. Hamilton's time in the valley was short-lived, as he went hunting that August and never returned. Signal Mountain earned its name after a search party was dispatched with instructions to light a fire on top of the mountain when he was found. Hamilton's unrecognizable body was found drowned in the Snake River—he was identified by his clothing, watch, and trout fly collection. Speculation swirled that either he had faked his death or Sargent had murdered him. This image shows Merymere, the cabin Sargent constructed with Hamilton.

Sargent's Bay, on the eastern shore of northern Jackson Lake, is named after John Dudley Sargent, a relative of famed artist John Singer Sargent. John D. Sargent was the son of a wealthy Maine man who paid him to go west and stay away from the family. It is not known why he was banished, but he arrived in Jackson Hole with his wife and five children and settled on the northernmost homestead in the valley. After building his home, Merymere, he began housing travelers. Sargent had a reputation among his friends for being mentally unstable. After the mysterious 1890 death of Sargent's land partner, Robert Ray Hamilton, Sargent's wife was found beaten to death in 1897. She had reportedly accused her husband of murdering Hamilton. Sargent was never tried due to lack of evidence, but while he was in jail, he was deemed insane and lost his children.

Sargent's second wife, Edith, who is shown playing the violin outside Merymere, had a history of mental illness. Her family paid Sargent to marry and take care of her. Edith had an unusual way of playing the violin—she would perch naked in a tree on the main trail going to Yellowstone National Park and make her music. She was eventually placed in a psychiatric hospital.

Sargent enjoyed sitting in his favorite rocking chair by the fireplace at Merymere. After his wife was taken away and the support from his family in Maine disappeared, Sargent committed suicide by shooting himself in the head with a rifle in this room.

Arthur Bradford, aka "Teton" Jackson, was perhaps the most notorious outlaw in the Teton basin. From 1878 to 1885, he and his gang of horse thieves drove horses from Utah, Nevada, and Idaho into the seclusion of the valley, where the criminals changed the horses' brands. The thieves then sold the horses to markets in Wyoming, South Dakota, and Montana.

In 1885, Johnson County sheriff Frank Canton captured Teton Jackson moving a herd of stolen horses through the Big Horn Mountains. Jackson was sentenced to prison in Boise, Idaho, and escaped in 1886 by tunneling out of his cell. He was recaptured in 1888. It is rumored that he buried his loot near Cache Creek, but it has never been recovered.

The above image shows a group of Bannock Indians, while the below image shows a group of Shoshone "Sheepeater" Indians. The Fort Bridger Treaty of 1868 displaced the Shoshone-Bannock Indians from Jackson Hole onto a reservation at Fort Hall, Idaho. The tribe was still allowed to hunt in occupied territory, as they relied on elk and other game for their sustenance. Unaware of state lines, they continued to cross into the valley to hunt elk. During the 1890s, "tuskers" began harvesting elk for their teeth. As big-game hunting emerged, tensions escalated between locals and the Bannocks. The elk herd was being harvested to near extinction and the Wyoming legislature passed a law banning the wanton killing of elk in the early 1890s. These were all precursors to the so-called Bannock War (or Bannock Uprising) of 1895.

In July 1895, a Bannock hunting party was arrested by a posse. The Bannocks were allowed to escape after conviction, since they could not afford to pay the fine and authorities could not afford to feed them. An old, blind Indian was killed during another confrontation, and more Indians were arrested for illegal hunting. Fearing retribution, residents of the valley banded together at Pierce Cunningham's ranch, pictured here. The women are unidentified.

The feared confrontation never arrived, but word spread to the East via telegraph and grew more and more exaggerated along the way. East Coast newspapers claimed that all white settlers in the valley had been massacred and every home set afire. Soldiers sent to help arrived to find everyone safe and accounted for—no marauding Indians and no fires. This illustration by Frederic Remington ran with a story about the "war" in the August 10, 1895, edition of *Harper's Weekly.*

Ed Harrington, aka Ed Trafton, is pictured here in a family portrait with his wife and three daughters. Trafton was arrested after rancher Hiram Lapham's cattle disappeared. Trafton escaped from jail after his wife smuggled a gun in by hiding it in their baby's clothing. He was recaptured and pardoned after only three years of a 25-year sentence. After his release, Trafton became the first postman for Teton Valley. While in this position he led a double life, robbing stores throughout the valley. He spent two more years in prison for the robberies, then turned his attention to the tourists in Yellowstone National Park. He is rumored to be responsible for holding up touring stagecoaches at gunpoint in 1908. He spent five years in prison after the infamous stagecoach robberies that earned him his nickname—the "lone highwayman of Yellowstone." On July 29, 1914, he single-handedly held up 15 stagecoaches at gunpoint, making off with $915.35 in cash and $130 in jewelry. W.C. "Slim" Lawrence discovered Trafton's well-concealed hideout cabin in the mountains in 1931.

Six

SETTLING THE VALLEY

Fur trappers, explorers, and prospectors began crisscrossing the Teton valley in the early 1800s, but none chose to brave the extreme winters and isolation on a permanent basis. That changed in 1884 with the arrival of John Holland and John Carnes and his wife, Millie—the first people intent on building a life in Jackson Hole. After these settlers arrived, they were followed by a slow trickle of predominantly male settlers. By 1888, there were 23 settlers in the area, including two women and one child.

The Homestead Act of 1862 fueled the settlement of the western United States. Pioneers hungry to own land set out to stake claims on public land. The Homestead Act required that the settler live on and cultivate up to 160 acres of land for five consecutive years. After five years, the settler had to file final proof papers for a fee of $15, then he or she owned the land. Conditions on the sagebrush flats of the valley floor were not ideal for cultivation or grazing of livestock. In some families, the wife filed an additional 160-acre claim so the family would have enough land to support themselves.

The majority of early settlers came to Jackson Hole from Idaho and Utah. In 1889, the state of Utah was drought-stricken, which led to a mass migration. Elijah "Uncle Nick" Wilson persuaded his family and four others to move to Jackson Hole. They were the first Mormons in Jackson Hole. New settlers who arrived in the valley throughout the 1890s were predominantly Mormon. Many of these families settled in the Antelope Flats area at the southern end of the park. This area is now known as Mormon Row.

Most early settlement occurred east of the Snake River, near the Gros Ventre River, and south of the current park boundary along Flat Creek. A few settlers did venture to the Spread Creek/ Buffalo Fork area in the northern end of the park, but none settled west of the Snake River until William D. Menor built a homestead there and began operating Menor's Ferry in 1894. It took almost 20 years for another settler to join him on the west side of the river.

John Carnes (left) settled in Teton country in 1884 with his Native American wife, Millie Sorelle, and his friend John Holland. The trio were the first settlers in the valley, making Millie the first woman to settle in the area. Carnes, pictured here in his Civil War uniform (he fought for the Union), was a trapper who had previously been to the area and returned to trap and pan for gold.

John Holland (right) arrived in the valley with John and Millie Carnes in 1884. The group started out from near Big Piney, Wyoming, and entered the valley via the Gros Ventre route. They dismantled their farm equipment and hauled it with packhorses. Some think they may have been the first settlers to bring a wagon over the Gros Ventre route.

In this image, John Holland leads his horse as it carries a bear Holland killed. Farming in the valley was difficult, and many homesteaders found other means to supplement their incomes. In addition to hunting and trapping, Holland served as the first justice of the peace in Jackson Hole and tried the valley's first case in 1892.

John Holland and John Carnes chose to homestead south of the Gros Ventre River in an area that produced lush hay and grasses. The land where Holland and Carnes built the first homestead in Jackson Hole was destined to become part of the National Elk Refuge; on August 10, 1912, Congress passed an act that set aside land for the refuge that included 34 homesteads.

Robert E. Miller (right) and his wife, Grace, pose on horseback in front of their homestead, which was located on land that is now part of the National Elk Refuge. In 1885, Miller became the first settler to bring a wagon into the valley via the Teton Pass. He dug ditches to irrigate his land and grazed the largest herd of cattle in the valley. He returned to Illinois to marry Grace in 1893 and brought her back to Jackson Hole, where he constructed this two-story home. Soon after Grace arrived in 1893, she acquired land next to her husband's so they could expand their cattle herd. By 1895, they grazed 126 head of cattle (the average herd was only 32 head), and within a few years, the herd had grown to 400 to 500 head. This house still stands on the National Elk Refuge today; at one time, it served as a temporary post office.

Over time, Robert and Grace Miller acquired more land and became one of the most influential couples in the valley. Grace platted land south of their homestead in 1897 and sold lots for the town of Jackson. Robert brought the first mowing machine into the valley by dismantling it to haul it over Teton Pass by packhorse. He loaned hay to neighboring homesteaders, which they paid back with interest, earning him the nickname "Old Twelve Percent." Robert later founded and was the first president of the Jackson State Bank. Through this position, he assisted the Snake River Land Company in the acquisition of property for the national park. He served as superintendent of Teton National Forest from 1908 to 1918. In 1920, Grace was elected mayor of Jackson and served with an all-female town council, earning them renown as the "Petticoat Government." The women elected were, from left to right, Mae Deloney, Rose Crabtree, Grace Miller, Faustina Haight, and Genevieve Van Vleck.

Martin "Slough Grass" Nelson (left) arrived in 1888 with his wife, Betty, and their daughter Cora. They claimed their homestead on the present-day site of National Elk Refuge near Flat Creek. He sold the homestead 10 years later because the land had become too swampy to farm. Lone pioneer Frank Wood preceded the Nelsons in 1886, but 1887 and 1888 brought several new settlers into the valley.

This image shows Bertha "Betty" Nelson, wife of Martin "Slough Grass" Nelson, and their daughters, Milliam (left) and Cora Barber. Betty was the second woman to arrive in the valley (after John Carnes's wife, Millie) and the first white woman to settle in the area. Cora was the first child brought to Jackson Hole.

Pioneers Dick Turpin (standing) and Frank Peterson take a break in this 1900 photograph. Turpin arrived in 1888 and homesteaded in the Flat Creek area. In 1892, he was charged with felonious assault and acquitted in the valley's first trial. Peterson settled in Jackson Hole in 1890 after visiting on a hunting excursion in 1889. He was a hunting guide and a member of the team that undertook the first documented ascent of the Grand Teton in 1898.

This 1900 image shows Emile Wolff outside his log cabin with his wife, Marie, and son Willie. Originally from Luxembourg, Emile first came to the valley in 1887 or 1888 and homesteaded near Flat Creek. He later returned to Europe to find a bride, and when they returned, they abandoned his original homestead for one north of Spread Creek.

John Pierce Cunningham arrived from New York in 1885, when he was about 20 years old. He made his living trapping until he filed a claim south of Spread Creek in 1888 under the Desert Land Act, which promoted the development of arid or semi-arid lands by requiring that the land be irrigated within three years of purchase at $1.25 per acre. Cunningham and his wife, Margaret, grazed 100 head of cattle and irrigated 140 acres, producing 75 tons of hay for winter feed. They were some of the first people to settle in the northern end of the park. Their original cabin was the site of the Affair at Cunningham's Ranch and the first Elk Post Office. Cunningham became one of the most prominent settlers of the area. He served as a justice of the peace and a game warden and was one of the original county commissioners when Teton County was established in 1923. He sold to the Snake River Land Company in 1928, but his cabin still stands in the park.

Elijah Nicholas Wilson (right), aka "Uncle Nick," brought his family and four other Mormon families to the valley in 1889. He grew up in Utah as one of 18 children living in hunger and poverty. He ran away from home to live with the Shoshone tribe of an Indian boy he had befriended. Chief Washakie's mother adopted him, giving him the name Yagaiki. He lived with the tribe for two years, learning their language and customs. Wilson was a colorful storyteller. His autobiography, *White Indian Boy: My Life Among the Shoshones*, was first published in 1910. Wilson published other books, too, and the 2000 movie *Wind River* was based on his story. The c. 1858 image below shows Wilson's adoptive brother Chief Washakie (center) with his wife Hanabi (right, holding their baby) and Nick's adoptive mother. (Below, photograph by William Henry Jackson.)

Nick Wilson's brother Sylvester Wilson (left) departed drought-stricken Utah looking for better land in the Snake River Valley of Idaho only to find no winter feed available for his livestock. Nick was returning from a trip to Jackson Hole and learned of Sylvester's situation. He convinced Sylvester that lush, native hay and plentiful water awaited them in Jackson Hole. In 1889, five families began the journey from Utah, including Nick's family and their daughter's family, Sylvester's family and his son Ervin Wilson's family, and Sylvester's son-in-law Selar Cheney's family.

The Wilson wagon train, pictured here coming into Jackson Hole, was the first to cross Teton Pass—it took two weeks pulling two wagons at a time for them to cross the pass. Their passage bolstered Teton Pass's reputation as a viable transportation route. This photograph was gifted to Jackson Hole Historical Society by Jimmy Goodrick.

Nick Wilson chose to homestead at the base of Teton Pass road at present-day Wilson, which is named after him. He held many occupations throughout his life, including Pony Express rider, stagecoach driver, trapper, blacksmith, carpenter, and frontier doctor. He was an Indian interpreter and was often called to negotiate peace with runaways from the reservation. Wilson was also a Mormon bishop and former prison guard. Ironically, he was jailed for cohabitation. Wilson is pictured at right with his three wives. The arrival of the Wilsons began the migration of many Mormon families into Jackson Hole in the 1890s. By 1900, 174 settlers had come from Utah—more than 25 percent of the valley's population. The above photograph was gifted to Jackson Hole Historical Society by Edna Bradford.

William D. (Bill) Menor (standing) was the first person to settle on the west side of the Snake River in 1892. His brother Holiday Menor (sitting) joined him in 1908, homesteading 160 acres on the east side of the river across from William's homestead. (Courtesy Dorothy Redmond Hubbard Collection.)

Bill Menor's homestead (pictured) was the only homestead on the west side of the Snake River until James Manges filed preemption papers in 1911. This view from the east side of the Snake River shows Menor's cabin behind the docked ferry with covered wagons and outbuildings in the background. (Photograph by Frank A. Hadsell.)

At right, Bill Menor stands next to his ferry. Early settlers had to ford the Snake River. This was extremely dangerous during periods of high water. Menor saw the need for a safer crossing and chose a spot near present-day Moose, Wyoming, where the river narrows into one channel. Two other ferries operated on the Snake River—one was near Oxbow Bend in the northern end of the park, and the other was south of the park at the crossing east of Teton Pass. The latter ferry was replaced by a steel truss bridge in 1915, but the approaches were wiped out by a flood in 1917. People traveled 20 miles out of the way to use Menor's Ferry to cross the Snake River until the bridge was reconstructed. The photograph below shows Menor's Ferry crossing the Snake River with horses and riders.

William Menor built his ferry to operate as a business, and it became the most important Snake River crossing along with the Jackson-Wilson Bridge. The sign above shows the rates Menor charged to board his ferry, from 25¢ for a foot traveler to $2 for a four-horse team and wagon. Menor operated the ferry during periods of high water and constructed a bridge for use during winter or periods of low water. When spring runoff from snowmelt overflowed the banks of the river, Menor would not risk himself, the ferry, or his passengers. In the early 1900s image below, two unidentified women, along with their horses and carriage, catch a ride on Menor's Ferry.

William Menor operated his ferry for over 20 years. In 1918, he sold the ferry and his homestead to Maud Noble, Frederick Sandell, and May Lee. After selling, Menor moved to San Diego. He was joined by his brother Holiday, who sold his homestead in 1928. Noble and Sandell doubled the ferry fare, angering valley residents, when automobile use increased.

Maud Noble and Frederick Sandell continued to operate the ferry until it was replaced by this steel truss bridge, known as the Moose-Wilson bridge. With the advent of the automobile, tourism had increased in the valley. In 1924, the Bureau of Public Roads decided to build a highway connecting Jackson with Menor's Ferry. After the bridge was completed in 1927, the ferry became obsolete, prompting Noble to open a tea room in her cabin.

This reenactment was held to celebrate the restoration of Menor's Ferry. The property was purchased by the Snake River Land Company as part of acquisitions for the future park in 1929. John D. Rockefeller Jr. had the ferry and buildings restored, then donated them to the National Park Service in 1953; the park service continues to maintain them. Note the whitewashed exterior of the cabin. Menor originally made his own whitewash with material from his brother Holiday's lime pit. In 1969, Menor's property was listed in the National Register of Historic Places. One of the most popular modern activities in the park is a scenic float down the Snake River. These guided tours depart from Pacific Creek Landing, near Moran, or Deadman's Bar, and take floaters on a winding path through spectacular views down the Snake River all the way to Menor's Ferry.

Charles and Maria Allen came from Rockland, Idaho. After Charles visited Jackson Hole in 1895, he returned home and convinced three other families to migrate to the valley. The families that joined the Allens were the James May family, the James A. Budge family, and the Roy McBride family. They entered the valley via the Teton Pass route, using two teams of horses to pull each wagon across the Tetons. The steep summit proved too much for two teams of horses, and they had to add a third team to get the wagons over the final incline. Charles and Maria stayed with John Carnes for the winter before settling at Moran, located between the outlet of Jackson Lake and the junction of Pacific Creek with the Snake River, to raise cattle. May and Budge were the first to settle 160-acre claims north of the Gros Ventre River and southeast of Blacktail Butte along what would become known as Mormon Row.

Like Charles and Maria Allen, Cap and Clara Smith also built a homestead near the outlet of Jackson Lake with the intent of raising cattle. Their homestead was located near the military route to Yellowstone and the Marysville Road to Idaho. They soon realized that catering to travelers would bring in additional income and constructed the Jackson Hotel (pictured).

The Jackson Hotel burned down sometime around 1900. After the hotel burned down, Charles and Maria Allen stepped in to fill the void for travelers and constructed the Elkhorn Hotel (pictured). The hotel included a roadhouse, a store, and a post office. The town of Moran received its name when Maria Allen opened the first post office in 1902.

This unidentified man (possibly Lee Lucas) is using the clothes wringer outside of the Lee Lucas homestead in winter. Lucas arrived in Jackson Hole in 1896. He settled in Spring Gulch and built a large cattle ranch. He eventually owned 640 acres of land, 450 head of cattle, and 50 horses.

The dry climate of the valley was not well suited to agriculture. As a result, many dug their own irrigation ditches, as this man is doing. Settlers in the Antelope Flats area repaired and took advantage of Mining Ditch, digging offshoots to supply water to their land. Mining Ditch was originally excavated by gold prospectors in 1870 or 1871.

Starting with James I. May in 1896, the remainder of the Charles and Maria Allen party from Rockland, Idaho, settled south and east of Blacktail Butte. From 1897 to 1899, others settled in the same area, including James Budge, Frank McBride, Nels Hoagland, Albert Nelson, Thomas Hanshaw, William S. Kissenger, Frank Sebastian, Joe Henrie, Martin Henrie, and Fred Lovejoy. The majority of the settlers were Mormon, and the area became known as Mormon Row. It is located within the park east of US Highway 89 and south of Antelope Flats Road. The buck-and-rail fence in the photograph was used by the first settlers. Constructed of lodgepole pine, it required no digging for post holes. Barbed wire was later added to some fencing, but when tourism became more popular, dude ranchers reverted to this older style of fencing, which is more aesthetically pleasing. The fencing is still prominent in the park today. The Mormon Row Historic District was listed in the National Register of Historic Places in 1997. This photograph was gifted to Jackson Hole Historical Society by Gertrude W. Brennan and Frank M. Brennan.

Andy Chambers claimed his homestead on Mormon Row in 1912, but his cabin was not completed until 1916. Chambers supplemented his cattle ranching income with trapping. From 1932 to 1940, he acquired the Jackson-Moran postal contract. The Andy Chambers Ranch Historic District was listed in the National Register of Historic Places in 1990. It is the only remaining homestead in the park today that is almost complete; the remaining buildings include the house, barn, garage, and outbuildings. Settlement continued on Mormon Row until approximately 1920. The Mormon leaders sent people from the Salt Lake Valley to establish new communities to support their growing population. The Mormon homesteaders who arrived in the valley stuck together and formed their own community, building cabins and houses on either side of a single road, which allowed for the best use of the land behind the homestead structures—this was considered a line village. The Mormons created a network of irrigation ditches, levees, and dikes. Some of these ditches still have water flowing through them today.

The three people above are in the process of harvesting grain with equipment pulled by horses. The below photograph shows George Riniker's grain fields after harvest on his Mormon Row homestead. Riniker claimed the homestead in 1912, after Pres. Theodore Roosevelt signed an executive order expanding Teton National Forest on July 1, 1908. This order opened previously closed lands in the valley to homesteading and brought a new wave of settlers to the area, including Thomas Murphy, Henry May, Albert Gunther, Joseph Eggleston, and Thomas Alma Moulton and his brother John. The Clifton May homestead buildings are barely visible behind the harvested grain field below. (Below, photograph by Floyd Naegeli.)

The T.A. Moulton barn (above), one of the most photographed barns in America, has become a symbol of Jackson Hole. In September 1908, Thomas Alma Moulton and his brother John took advantage of the executive order releasing new lands and claimed neighboring homesteads on Antelope Flats along Mormon Row. They first built the barn in 1913 as a square structure. Over time, it evolved into the barn as it looks today. The Moultons worked their farm until 1961; the barn is all that remains of their homestead. The John Moulton homestead (below) sits just north of Antelope Flats Road. He kept dairy cattle in the barn, selling milk and cream to nearby ranches. The Moultons were joined by another brother, Wallace, in 1909. The John Moulton barn is often mistaken for the T.A. Moulton barn. (Above, photograph by Olie Riniker.)

Norman Smith and his wife are pictured here in 1912 on their homestead northwest of Blacktail Butte. Two early parties of settlers found themselves staying in the valley due to misfortune. The Smith family pulled up their roots in Cody, Wyoming, and set out for Colorado in 1907. Their route took them through Yellowstone National Park into Jackson Hole. When they were in the valley, one of their horses died, and their daughter became ill. They deliberated and decided to stay, purchasing the homestead on which they had camped. Earlier settlers Noble Gregory and his father, Samuel, arrived in Jackson Hole after becoming lost. Bound for Idaho, they traveled by wagon over South Pass and somehow lost their map. A wrong turn north along the west side of the Wind River Range eventually resulted in their arrival in the valley after they followed the Gros Ventre River. They nixed their plans for Idaho and claimed a homestead in the Buffalo Fork area in 1898.

In this early 1900s image, Mary Wadams stands in the doorway of her sod-roofed cabin. Most cabins of the time were only one or two rooms with one door and one window. They were constructed with lodgepole pine logs and had dirt floors that were dampened and swept until they became hard. Wadams hung white muslin on the ceiling of her cabin to reflect light and catch dirt from the roof.

The Charles and Delilah Hedrick homestead was located approximately three miles south of Spread Creek. They were among the settlers who took advantage of Pres. Theodore Roosevelt's executive order that opened up the lands in the area to settlement in 1908. Today, Hedrick Pond marks the location of the Hedrick homestead.

In this c. 1910 image, Henrietta West Neal is feeding the chickens on the Neal homestead in the Buffalo River Valley in northern Jackson Hole. The Neal family's log cabin is in the background. Note that it is built in the same cabin style as the Wadams cabin. Many settlers added floor boards over dirt floors as soon as the first sawmills made lumber available in the valley.

In 1911, James Manges (pictured) ended William Menor's solitary existence on the west side of the Snake River. He filed preemption papers on 160 acres near the confluence of Cottonwood and Taggart Creeks at the base of the Tetons. Manges built the first two-story cabin in the area with an overhanging roof to shed snow. His cabin is listed in the National Register of Historic Places. (Photograph by S.C. Holz.)

In this 1917 photograph, Harriet (left) and Jimmy Braman pull a dog in their wagon on the Frank Braman homestead. Braman homesteaded 160 acres on Pacific Creek. After the postwar depression and losing his crop to severe drought in 1919, he did not replant the following year. In 2011, bidders paid a combined total of $3,685,000 for only 4.8 acres of his former ranch land.

This group of homesteaders is harvesting and threshing the first crop of oats at the Timmins homestead. Settlers in the valley often pooled their resources and united to help each other through the harvest. Homesteaders tended to settle next to others, and small communities of neighbors began to form, creating the basis for the area's first towns.

Ed "Roan Horse (Roanie)" Smith is pictured at left with his dog on the porch of his homestead cabin near Cottonwood Creek at the base of the Tetons. In 1921, Smith homesteaded 160 acres at Lupine Meadows on a relinquishment homestead that had an existing cabin on it. Smith was 54 years old when he took out the homestead with the stated intention of breeding horses, although some thought it was really his retirement place. Below, settlers with snowshoes visit Roanie at his cabin. They are, from left to right, Geraldine Lucas, Tony Grace, Hildegarde Crandall, Lida Gabbey, Leonard Timmermeyer, Albert Gabbey, and Harrison R. Crandall. (Below, photograph by Harrison Crandall.)

Seven

THE VALLEY'S FIRST TOWNS

The arrival of John Carnes and John Holland in 1884 opened up a slow stream of settlers arriving in Jackson Hole through the end of the 19th century. They settled the best agricultural and ranching lands close to transportation routes and spread out from there. As time went on, four major areas of the valley grew from small communities to towns: Jackson, in southern Jackson Hole; Wilson, at the base of Teton Pass; Moran, at the outlet of Jackson Lake toward the northern end of the valley; and Kelly, along the Gros Ventre River. Smaller communities like Zenith, Antler, and Elk never flourished and no longer exist.

Often, the first sign that a small community had formed was the opening of a local post office. Early post offices were operated out of homestead cabins or existing businesses and sometimes moved from one location to another. In 1892, the Marysvale post office became the first to open in Jackson Hole. It was operated out of the Fred White homestead and named after Fred's wife, Mary. When the Whites moved from their homestead in 1894, William and Maggie Simpson took over the post office, and it was renamed Jackson. With its superior geographic accessibility to the Teton and South Pass transportation routes, Jackson emerged as the valley's dominant community.

Demand for goods and services grew along with the population. Settlers needed access to everyday essentials, building supplies, farm equipment, dry goods, blacksmiths, doctors, and other services. Entrepreneurs built the valley's first businesses to meet these needs. The frontier, once filled with bachelors, now contained families who needed access to schools and churches. Traffic into the valley gradually increased, and enterprising individuals built the first hotels to accommodate weary travelers. Over time, Jackson Hole's economic base began to switch from agriculture and cattle ranching to accommodating incoming tourists. Today, the tourist industry is the backbone of the valley's economy.

This group of men is standing outside of Charles "Pap" Deloney's general mercantile store and home. Deloney realized the need for a reliable supply of goods for the valley's settlers, and in 1899, he built the valley's first general mercantile store in the town of Jackson. His wife, Claire, served as the valley's midwife and doctor.

Abraham Ward (right) stands with his wife, Edna, and daughter in front of the Wilson Hotel, which they operated. In 1898, Ward built the hotel, a saloon, and a store with the help of his father-in-law, Nick Wilson. The town of Wilson took hold below the Teton Pass transportation route; since it was on the west side of the Snake River, it had trouble thriving in its early days.

The above image shows Ben Sheffield (riding on the horse) hauling wood for Jackson Lake Lodge. In 1903, Sheffield purchased two homesteads at the Snake River outlet of Jackson Lake and built the Teton Lodge Resort for his hunting and tourist business. He built a toll bridge (below) across the Snake River, making the town of Moran a transportation link for travelers. Moran was the first tourist town in the valley, as its economy relied solely on the tourism industry. The construction of the Jackson Lake Dam brought workers and new construction to the town. The Snake River Land Company acquired Moran for the park in 1929.

The original Jackson Lake Dam (pictured above with Moran in the background) was a log cofferdam constructed in 1906–1907. It failed in 1910, and construction began on a new dam (below), which is still in use today. The new dam took six years to complete. The original dam had raised the level of Jackson Lake 22 feet. The new dam—part of the Minidoka Project to provide irrigation from the Snake River to farms in Idaho—raised the level 30 feet. When Grand Teton National Park was created in 1929, it did not include Jackson Lake; purists fought to have the lake excluded because it was no longer a natural lake. (Below, photograph by Floyd Bous.)

Charlie Fessler's store in Moran, pictured above around 1924, was the only place in northern Jackson Hole for tourists to purchase gasoline. The gas and supplies for the store were freighted in from Ashton, Idaho, via the old Reclamation Road by Flagg Ranch. Since no railroads traveled into Jackson Hole, freighters brought goods into the valley via wagons pulled by teams of horses. Materials for the Jackson Lake Dam were also delivered this way. Below, freighter Ray H. Osborne brings his team, led by horses Star (left) and Bally, across Pilgrim Creek as Mount Moran rises in the background. Osborne brought the last horse-drawn freight outfit into the valley from Ashton to Moran.

By the turn of the 20th century, more families populated the valley, and rural schoolhouses began to become a priority. These children are at school in Zenith with teacher Eva Phillips (Lucas) standing behind the children (in the center of the photograph). Wyoming senator Clifford Hansen was from the tiny town of Zenith, which no longer exists.

Practicing faith was important to valley residents. In 1905, the Mormons built the first church in Jackson. In the image below, two unidentified women stand outside the church in Grovont (the town's name changed to Kelly in 1909), which was completed in 1913 by Rev. Seth Hawley. In later years, the building housed a store. (Courtesy of Rev. Seth Hawley's daughter.)

Kelly was originally named Grovont by the US Postal Service. The postal service preferred one-word town names, so they combined Gros Ventre into the French pronunciation of the words. It was typical for early post offices to be operated out of the homestead of the postmaster, so the Grovont post office moved around on Mormon Row. It is pictured at the Andy Chambers homestead.

The school, church, and rectory were the only buildings in Kelly that survived the flood on May 17, 1927, when the dam holding Lower Slide Lake broke loose. After the flood, the post office was temporarily housed at the Bark residence (right). Relaxing outside are, from left to right, Anne Kent, Raymond Kent, Donald Kent, Leola Clark, two unidentified men, and Walter Woodward.

In this c. 1920 photograph, early settlers Charles and Maria Allen stand next to a car in front of the Kelly Drugstore and post office. In 1902, Maria served as the first postmaster for the town of Moran, where she ran the post office out of the family's Elkhorn Hotel. The Allens came to the area from Rockland, Idaho, in 1896.

Although the valley was a peaceful place, a growing population necessitated increased law enforcement. James A. Francis served as sheriff of Teton County from 1923 to 1943. He is pictured at left on horseback wearing his sheriff's star. Francis was also a successful cattle rancher in the Spring Gulch area of southern Jackson Hole.

Standing outside the Jenny Lake school bus (a horse-drawn sled) in 1941 are, from left to right, Ed "Roan Horse" Smith, Lew Smith, and Lida Gabbey. Gabbey was the teacher at Jenny Lake School and the Jenny Lake postmaster when the office opened in 1926 to serve tourists. The Smiths had the school sled contract and transported children from Moran to Moose. Transportation in wintertime was a challenge in Jackson Hole, as average snowfall amounts on the valley floor vary from 66 inches at the southern end of the valley to 160 inches (and more) toward the northern end. Higher mountain elevations receive over 450 inches of snow each year. Other popular modes of winter transportation included dogsleds, skis, and snowshoes. Below, Jack Kranenberg gives his dogsled team a break in front of a gas station and store.

At left, Harrison Crandall's niece Esther leans on a sign advertising the String Lakes Pavilion in 1925. Harrison Crandall built the dance pavilion to supplement his income after he and his wife Hildegarde decided to homestead east of String Lake in 1924, taking out a stock-raising entry for 40 head of horses. The pavilion was a 70-foot-long log structure with a plank floor. Hildegarde spent her weekdays cooking and baking for the midnight supper served at the weekly dance. The dances entertained locals and tourists, with the *Jackson's Hole Courier* reporting 250 guests at the first dance. Harrison tore down the pavilion after just two years and used the logs to build his photography studio (below). (Left, photograph by Harrison Crandall.)

Eight

RANCHERS AND TOURISM

Almost all early Jackson Hole settlers became cattle ranchers. Some tried their hands at raising crops, but the climate and soil were not well suited for agriculture. The climate was also not suited to year-round open-range grazing due to the harsh winter months, so the settlers used the practice of mountain valley ranching. Ranchers would turn their herds out to graze during the summer and fall, then bring them back home for protection from the cold and snow. The size of the herd was dependent on the amount of hay they were able to cultivate for winter feed during the short growing season.

Few early ranchers relied solely on ranching for income. Most took other jobs to make ends meet. One resource the valley had in abundance was big game. Big-game hunters were the first true tourists to come to the valley. Enterprising ranchers capitalized on this by offering guide services to hunters and fishermen. With the depressed cattle market of the 1920s, ranchers looked to wealthy city dwellers willing to pay handsomely for an Old West experience. This ushered in the age of the dude wranglers, and ranchers built barebones cabins to accommodate guests. Dudes wanted an authentic cowboy experience. It was not until the 1930s that some ranches installed electricity and plumbing for guests. In addition to guided hunts, pack trips, and ranch work, ranchers entertained dudes with costume parties, dances, and rodeos.

Driving tours and vacations became increasingly popular as more and more people were able to afford automobiles. The lure of the scenic mountains—with their climbing and skiing challenges, wildlife, fishing, and proximity to Yellowstone National Park—continued to increase tourist traffic into the valley. The uncertainties of farming and ranching gave way to the tourist economy, and now, more than three million people visit the park each year.

This cowboy on the Elk Ranch is possibly bringing the herd into its winter enclosure. The 160 acres allowed under the Homestead Act of 1862 and additional 160 under the Desert Land Act of 1891 did not provide enough acreage for grazing large herds of cattle. The Stock-Raising Act of 1916 increased the allowed acreage to 640, and herd sizes grew.

These riders are heading out on a pack trip from the Stephen Leek Ranch in South Park. The Leek Ranch and Leek's Camp on Jackson Lake are considered by some historians to be the first dude ranch in Jackson Hole. (Courtesy Stephen Leek Collection, American Heritage Center, University of Wyoming.)

Stephen N. Leek (right) holds a mackinaw trout as he stands on the shore of Jackson Lake with an unidentified man. Leek arrived in Jackson Hole in 1888 and established himself as a hunting and fishing guide. In 1927, he built cabins and a lodge to provide outdoor experiences for boys—Leek's Camp was located near the present-day site of Leek's Marina.

Hunters rest with their elk antlers and bear pelts at one of Leek's hunting camps. Although Leek was a hunter, he abhorred the wanton killing of elk for their eyeteeth and was instrumental in establishing the National Elk Refuge. (Courtesy Stephen Leek Collection, American Heritage Center, University of Wyoming.)

Early settlers John Holland (above, far left) and Cal Carrington (above, far right) pose with unidentified hunters displaying their trophies. Carrington was a hunting guide rumored to have been a horse thief before settling near Sheep Mountain. He told people he had no name. On a hunt he was guiding, a wealthy English hunter named Carrington asked his name, and he replied that he did not have one. Further prompting revealed he had run away from his adoptive father and refused to be known by the man's name. The Englishman gave Carrington his surname and suggested Cal for a first name, as the guide frequently talked about going to California. Not all early hunters were men, as shown by the unidentified woman below standing over her bull elk kill.

Improvements in transportation made it possible for more people to visit Jackson Hole. The first automobile arrived in the valley, driven by tourists over Togwotee Pass, in 1908. Togwotee Pass (its 1921 dedication is pictured above) became one of the main routes to Grand Teton and Yellowstone National Parks. The first airplane (below) to fly into Jackson Hole arrived on August 19, 1920, piloted by H.H. Barker. Local businessmen saw the airplane as an opportunity to expand winter sports. A small airstrip located at the Jackson rodeo grounds served as an airport until 1946, when construction was completed on a commercial airport southwest of Blacktail Butte. Jackson Hole Airport is the only airport within a national park and is now the busiest airport in Wyoming.

Louis Joy is pictured in 1901 on horseback at the future site of his JY Ranch. In 1908, Joy and Struthers Burt started the first dude ranch in Jackson Hole, according to the definition set forth by the Dude Ranchers' Association established in 1926. Guests enjoyed horseback riding, pack trips, hunting, fishing, and swimming (in nearby Phelps Lake). After the property was purchased for the park in 1932, it became the Rockefeller family's retreat.

C-15 Bar BC Reflections   Crandall

Struthers Burt broke off his partnership with Louis Joy and opened the Bar BC with Horace Carncross in 1912. The ranch became one of the most well-known in the West in the golden age of dude ranching from 1919 to 1929. Dude ranchers did not accept overnight travelers, and many, like the Bar BC, required potential guests to present references. (Photograph by Harrison Crandall.)

Some dudes fell in love with the Tetons and never left. Polish countess Eleanor "Cissy" Patterson Gizycka (right) purchased Cal Carrington's ranch after a stay at the Bar BC. Carrington stayed on to run the ranch, and the two were rumored to be romantically involved. Owen Wister, author of *The Virginian*, first visited the JY Ranch with his family in 1911. In 1912, he purchased a 160-acre homestead for a ranch along today's Moose-Wilson Road. Wealthy associates from his native Philadelphia were his main clientele. Wister sold the property in 1920, and it became the R Lazy S dude ranch. When the property became part of Grand Teton National Park, the house (below) was dismantled and moved from the R Lazy S to Medicine Bow, Wyoming.

In 1913 and 1915, Harold Hammond and George Tucker Bispham, intent on cattle ranching, took up neighboring homesteads near Buck Mountain and formed a partnership. Their plans were interrupted when Hammond enlisted in the Army at the start of World War I. Upon his return, the partners built the White Grass Ranch lodge (pictured above), cabins, and a rare, concrete-lined swimming pool and began dude wrangling instead of cattle ranching.

The White Grass Ranch may have experienced financial difficulties. In 1924, Hammond and Bispham sold to the Bar BC but continued managing the ranch until 1928, when they purchased it back. After buying back the ranch, they started the White Grass Silver Black Fox Ranch, raising silver foxes (left) for the fur industry. The White Grass was an operating dude ranch until 1985.

Dudes came from the city to get an authentic cowboy experience at the Jackson Hole ranches. In addition to hunting and horseback riding, they often did work on the ranch. The dudes sitting on the fence are watching Triangle X ranch hands brand cattle.

Fred (kneeling at left) and Eva Topping (kneeling at center) opened the Moosehead Ranch in 1937. They also operated a fox and mink farm. These guests are enjoying dinner cooked over the campfire. In 1932, the Elk Post Office moved to the Moosehead, and Eva was the postmaster until it closed in 1967. The ranch is still in operation today.

The Elbo Ranch was located south of Jenny Lake and west of the Snake River at the base of the Teton Range. It was advertised as a dude ranch by partners Chester Goss, J.M. Goss, and James G. Scott but operated more as a tourist accommodation and entertainment facility. The facility included cabins, a store, a gas station, and rodeo grounds complete with a grandstand and racetrack. The Elbo Rodeo provided popular entertainment for guests of the local dude ranches. Above, the Bar BC Stage brings dudes to the Elbo Rodeo around 1925. Below, onlookers and participants enjoy the greased pig contest at the rodeo.

Above, a man stands on the porch at the Moose Store and gas station, with horses at left and cars at the pumps. The store sign advertised "Tackle for Fly Fishermen." Although it had a post office, Moose was never a true town—it developed as an area that catered to passing tourists. Below, dudes are going to church at the Chapel of the Transfiguration sometime in the 1930s. The chapel was built in 1925. The window behind the altar frames the Cathedral Group of the Tetons. Dornan's, at Moose, started out of Evelyn Dornan's home and grew into the tourist complex of restaurants, accommodations, and activities that it is today. The new Craig Thomas Discovery & Visitor Center and Menor's Ferry are also located at Moose. (Above, courtesy Hartgrave Collection.)

In this c. 1927 image, Jack Knori (left) and Slim Lawrence stand outside the Jenny Lake Inn. Like Moose, Jenny Lake was not a true town but rather a collection of tourist businesses located on popular Jenny Lake. It offered a gas station and store, equipment rentals for outdoor activities, boat rentals, and mountain climbing guided by Glenn Exum and Paul Petzoldt.

The ski party pictured here in 1929 includes, from left to right, Jack Berry, Walt Feuz, Mattie Piquet, Noble Gregory, Bert Turner, Frank Coffin, and Carlos Johnson. Winter sports that had previously only been enjoyed by locals attracted tourists soon after the first airplane flew into Jackson Hole in 1920, making it easier for visitors to arrive in winter.

PHOTO. BY W.O. OWEN, 1898.

John Shive (at left above), Franklin Spalding (center), Frank Peterson, and William Owen (not shown because he was taking the photograph) made the first documented ascent of the Grand Teton on August 11, 1898. A lull in climbing lasted for about 25 years until Horace Albright contacted mountaineering clubs in hopes of raising support for his national park proposal. As the sport grew in popularity, more climbers ventured to the Grand Tetons. Eleanor Davis became the first woman to climb the Grand Teton in 1923. She was followed by Geraldine Lucas (pictured at left with Jack Crawford sitting near her feet) in 1924, the first local woman to ascend the Grand Teton, which she did at the age of 59. Today, the Grand Tetons are considered a premier climbing destination in the United States. (Above, photograph by William O. Owen; left, photograph by Harold P. Fabian.)

Nine

THE BIRTH OF GRAND TETON NATIONAL PARK

From the first time Gen. Philip Sheridan voiced the idea of expanding Yellowstone National Park in 1882, the idea met with opposition and controversy. Charles D. Walcott echoed Sheridan's sentiments, proposing Teton National Park in 1898. In addition to protecting the elk herd, Walcott was a visionary who realized that the pristine beauty of the Tetons and Jackson Hole, combined with the unique features of Yellowstone, was the trip of a lifetime that should be preserved for future generations. The primary concern of early park expansionists was the fate of the elk herd, which they feared would be hunted to extinction.

Elk conservationists won their first battle when Congress passed an act that created the National Elk Refuge in 1912. Early settler and hunting guide Stephen Leek led the fight for the elk refuge. Although Leek was an avid hunter, he respected the herd and abhorred the indiscriminate killing of the animal by tusk hunters. Biologist Olaus Murie, along with his wife, Margaret (Mardy), arrived to study the elk herd in 1927. These strong conservation advocates joined the fight for park expansion and rallied with others for the creation of Jackson Hole National Monument.

Even before the Muries arrived, Stephen Mather and Horace Albright had been working diligently since 1916 to have the Teton Range and a portion of the valley designated as a national park. By 1923, some Jackson Hole locals had started to support the idea. A meeting of supporters at Maud Noble's cabin resulted in the Jackson Hole Plan. The need for private individuals to purchase and donate land for the park was a key element of the plan. The solution started to become clear in 1924, when Albright led John D. Rockefeller Jr. on a trip through Jackson Hole and told the wealthy businessman his dreams for the national park. In 1926, Rockefeller returned with his wife, Abigail, who also fell in love with the area and its majestic expanses of untouched nature. Rockefeller returned home and formed the Snake River Land Company to purchase over 33,000 acres of land, which he later donated to the federal government for the express purpose of creating Grand Teton National Park.

In 1931, John D. Rockefeller Jr. and his wife Abigail celebrated their 30th wedding anniversary at Jenny Lake. The Rockefellers were dedicated to preserving the pristine beauty of the Grand Tetons and Jackson Hole. Buildings and telephone wires disrupting the view of the mountains were not acceptable to the Rockefellers and were removed after the couple purchased the land for the park.

As early as 1921, local rancher Si Ferrin (center, with two unidentified riders) voiced his opinion in favor of park expansion by either private or government funding. Economic conditions worsened in the valley in the early 1920s, and more ranchers started to favor park expansion. In 1925, Ferrin and Pierce Cunningham circulated a petition in favor of seeking private funds to buy out local ranchers. (Photograph by the Schofield Brothers.)

Concern over commercial exploitation of Jackson Hole brought locals, who had been against the idea of park expansion at first, together with Horace Albright. The united front that formed the Jackson Hole Plan at Maud Noble's cabin (pictured) on July 26, 1923, included Noble, Dick Winger, Struthers Burt, Joe Jones, Horace Carncross, Jack Eynon, and Albright. The plan proposed seeking private funds to purchase land for the park.

This image shows Horace Albright meeting with members of the Snake River Land Company and others. Pictured are, from left to right, two unidentified men, Kenneth Chorley, Secretary of the Interior Ray Lyman Wilbur, Harold Fabian, and Albright. John D. Rockefeller Jr. formed the Snake River Land Company in 1927 for the purpose of purchasing land for the future park. (Photograph by Harrison Crandall gifted to Jackson Hole Historical Society by Herb and Quita Pownall.)

Above, Horace Albright is speaking at the dedication ceremony for Grand Teton National Park on July 29, 1929. A portion of his dream had come to fruition when Pres. Calvin Coolidge declared the Teton Range a national park on February 26, 1929. Albright would realize his entire dream when the park expansion of 1950 encompassed the lakes and portions of the valley. In connection with the ceremony, Dr. Fritiof Fryxell (below, left), Phil Smith, and William Gilman (not pictured because he was taking the photograph) ascended the Grand Teton to place a bronze plaque honoring the climbers who made the first documented ascent of the Grand Teton on August 11, 1898. The longstanding dispute about who made the first ascent was settled by a unanimous vote of the Wyoming legislature. (Below, photograph by William Gilman.)

The first ranger staff of Grand Teton National Park posed for this photograph in the summer of 1930. From left to right are Dr. Fritiof Fryxell, Phil Smith, Edward Bruce, Sam Woodring, Howard Sherman, Tom Secrest, and unidentified. Horace Albright appointed Woodring the superintendent of the newly created park. (Photograph by Harrison Crandall.)

This c. 1920 photograph shows game warden Charlie Peterson sitting in the doorway of a tusker cabin. In 1897, the superintendent of Yellowstone National Park, Col. S.B.M. Young, saw the need to protect the elk herd from tuskers and asked for expanded jurisdiction over Jackson Hole because he could not protect the herd outside of Yellowstone's boundaries.

Above, tusker Charles Purdy and an unidentified tusker stand outside of Purdy's cabin on Loon Lake. Tuskers killed elk for their eyeteeth, which were used for jewelry; most often, they were mounted on watch fobs for Elks Club badges. A pair of elk teeth could fetch between $10 and $25 (sometimes more)—enough to lure many hunters into the trade. When the Elks Club became aware of the wanton slaughter of elk for this purpose, it discontinued the use of elk teeth and became strong advocates for protection of the elk. The tusker smokehouse shown below was located on Glade Creek. Both Purdy's cabin and this smokehouse were conveniently located near the Ashton Freight Road. After smoking the elk meat, tuskers took it by packhorse via the Ashton Freight Road for sale in Idaho.

Stephen Leek (above), the driving force behind the creation of the National Elk Refuge, was known as the "Father of the Elk." Wire fencing trapped the elk in Jackson Hole, where there was not enough winter feed to support them, and prevented them from migrating to their usual winter feeding grounds. This, along with overextensive hunting, reduced the herd from 50,000 to 10,000 by 1911. Leek took countless pictures of the dead and starving elk, wrote articles, and went on a lecture tour to gain support for the elk's plight. On August 10, 1912, Congress created the National Elk Refuge, located just south of the park. Today, the refuge encompasses 24,700 acres. The Miller homestead (below) was incorporated into the refuge along with 33 other homesteads. (Above, photograph by the Schofield Brothers; below, photograph by K.F. Roahen.)

This c. 1936 image shows the Civilian Conservation Corps cleaning up dead trees along the shore of Jackson Lake. After the creation of the park, federal funding brought new roads, trails, and other infrastructure to the area. The construction of the Jackson Lake Dam had flooded and killed thousands of acres of trees in the 1910s, and this environmental eyesore was finally able to be cleaned up after 20 years.

Horace Albright and John D. Rockefeller Jr. continued to experience difficulty expanding the park. They proposed a national monument instead, which could be proclaimed by executive order under the Antiquities Act of 1906. Actor Wallace Beery (center), who had purchased land in the valley, and a group of ranchers protested the monument, because ranchers were concerned the monument would restrict their grazing rights.

Dr. Fritiof M. Fryxell, pictured here on a Teton mountain summit, was a geologist and avid mountain climber who conquered many of the range's peaks. He arrived in the Tetons in the summer of 1926 to complete field work for his dissertation on mountain glaciation. He was appointed the park's first naturalist in 1929 by Horace Albright.

Fryxell spent six summers as the park's naturalist. He was passionate about preserving the history of the early explorers and artists of the Tetons and founded the park's first museum. He spent countless hours climbing and exploring the Teton Range, developed an interpretive curriculum for visitors, and published *The Tetons: Interpretations of a Mountain Landscape* in 1938. In this image, Fryxell is on a climb overlooking Leigh Lake. (Photograph by Carl Blaurock.)

Husband and wife Olaus and Margaret "Mardy" Murie were local campaigners for the creation of the Jackson Hole National Monument and a driving force behind conservation in the valley. Olaus was a naturalist and biologist assigned to research the elk herd for the biological survey in 1927. He authored numerous publications, including *The Elk of North America* and *Jackson Hole with a Naturalist*. Olaus later became president of the Wilderness Society, Wildlife Society, and director of the Izaak Walton League of America. Mardy was known as the "Grandmother of the Conservation Movement." In addition to her conservation work in the Tetons, Murie helped with the passage of the Wilderness Act and the creation of the Arctic National Wildlife Refuge. She was the recipient of many awards over her lifetime, including the Audubon Medal, John Muir Award, and the Presidential Medal of Freedom (in 1998). In 2002, she was awarded the National Wildlife Federation's highest honor, the J.N. Ding Darling Conservationist of the Year Award, just before her 100th birthday. The Murie Ranch, located in Moose, Wyoming, is now home to the Murie Center, a conservation institute.

Above, Charles Allen and an unidentified hunter (possibly Roy McBride) stand over a mountain lion they killed. Due to the efforts of many individuals over many years, scenes like the one above and below are now nonexistent in Grand Teton National Park. Despite opposition, Pres. Franklin D. Roosevelt used his executive power and created Jackson Hole National Monument on March 15, 1943, encompassing the current park boundaries and the National Elk Refuge. Below, Roy McBride poses with his wolf pelts. Wolves were hunted to extinction in Jackson Hole by the early 1900s. They were reintroduced to Yellowstone National Park in 1995. There are now several packs in Jackson Hole, with the Huckleberry Pack living almost entirely within the park boundaries. (Above, photograph by Billy Bierer.)

Pres. Franklin D. Roosevelt set the stage by establishing Jackson Hole National Monument in 1943, and on December 16, 1949, John D. Rockefeller Jr. gifted 33,562 acres of land he had purchased to the federal government. On September 13, 1950, Pres. Harry Truman signed the bill establishing the Grand Teton National Park as it is known today. The National Elk Refuge stands on its own. Wildlife, like the grizzly bears pictured below, are free to roam the park and cause traffic jams when spotted by delighted visitors. Many different organizations and individuals work to maintain the park's pristine beauty and wildlife for future generations. The Murie Center continues to promote wilderness and wildlife conservation in Jackson Hole and around the world. Their mission statement reads: "Bringing people together to inspire action that preserves nature." Amen. (Right, photograph by Hayden Studio.)

DISCOVER THOUSANDS OF LOCAL HISTORY BOOKS FEATURING MILLIONS OF VINTAGE IMAGES

Arcadia Publishing, the leading local history publisher in the United States, is committed to making history accessible and meaningful through publishing books that celebrate and preserve the heritage of America's people and places.

Find more books like this at
www.arcadiapublishing.com

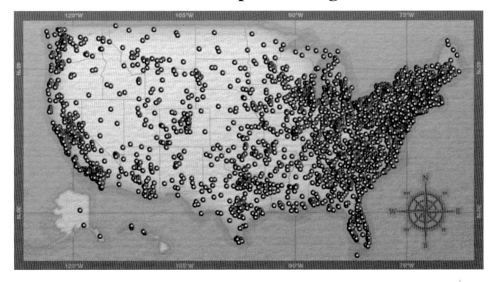

Search for your hometown history, your old stomping grounds, and even your favorite sports team.

Consistent with our mission to preserve history on a local level, this book was printed in South Carolina on American-made paper and manufactured entirely in the United States. Products carrying the accredited Forest Stewardship Council (FSC) label are printed on 100 percent FSC-certified paper.

MADE IN THE
USA